Helping Children See Jesus

ISBN: 978-1-64104-057-0

Believers in Christ
God's Workmanship
New Testament Volume 29: Ephesians

Author: R. Iona Lyster
Illustrator: Frances H. Hertzler
Computer Graphic Artist: Yuko Willoughby
Typesetting and Layout: Patricia Pope

© 2018 Bible Visuals International
PO Box 153, Akron, PA 17501-0153
Phone: (717) 859-1131
www.biblevisuals.org

All rights reserved. No part of this publication may be reproduced, stored in a retrieval system or transmitted in any form by any means, electronic, mechanical, photocopy, recording or otherwise, without the prior permission of the publisher, except as provided by USA copyright law.

RELATED ITEMS

To access related items (such as activities, memory verse posters and translated texts) please visit our web store at shop.biblevisuals.org and enter 1029 in the search box on the page.

FREE TEXT DOWNLOAD

To access a FREE printable copy of the teaching text (PDF format) in English or other available languages, enter S1029DL in the search box. Add the item to your cart, and use coupon code XTACSV17 at checkout. Once your order is processed you will receive an email with a link to the free download.

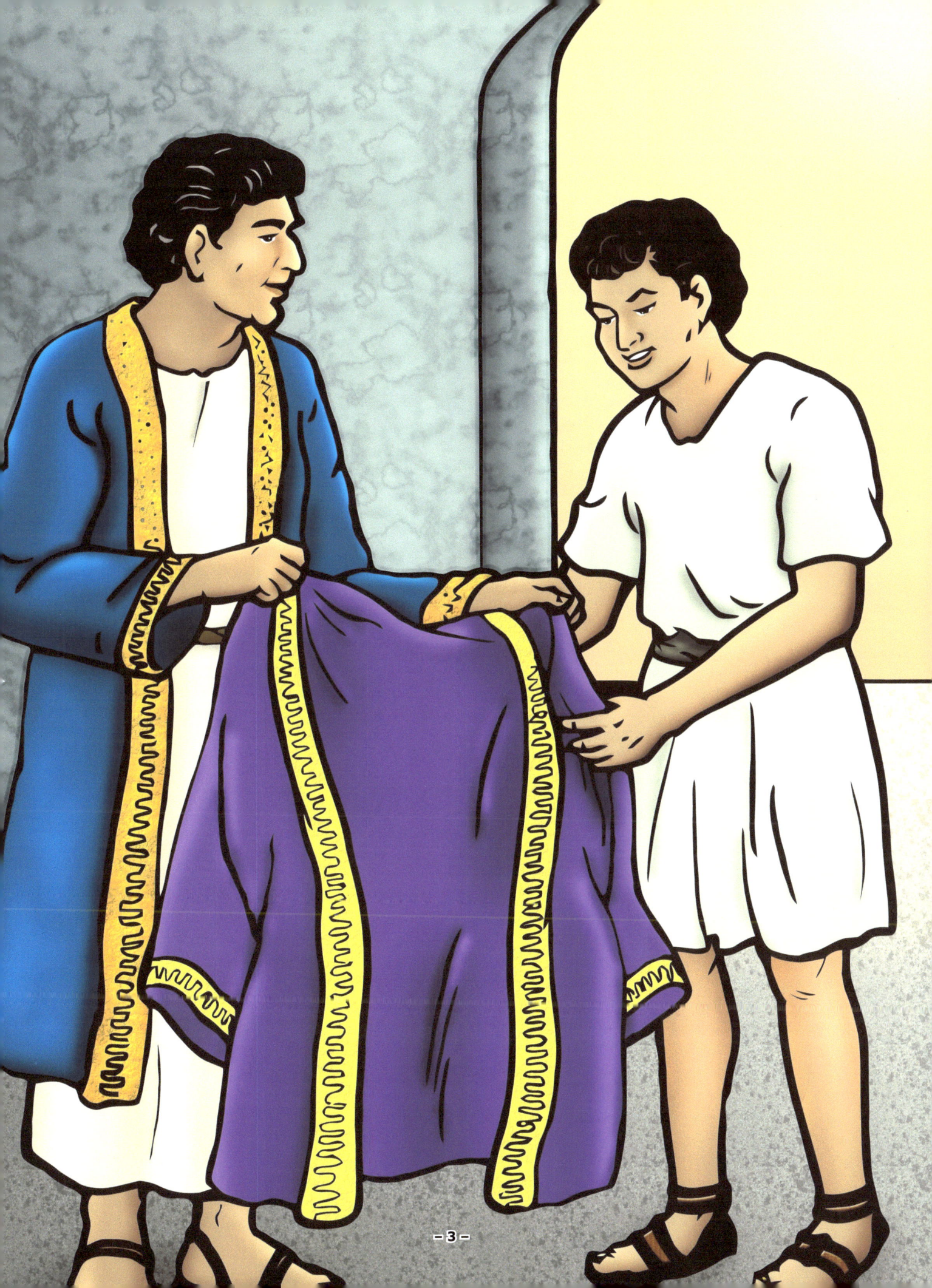

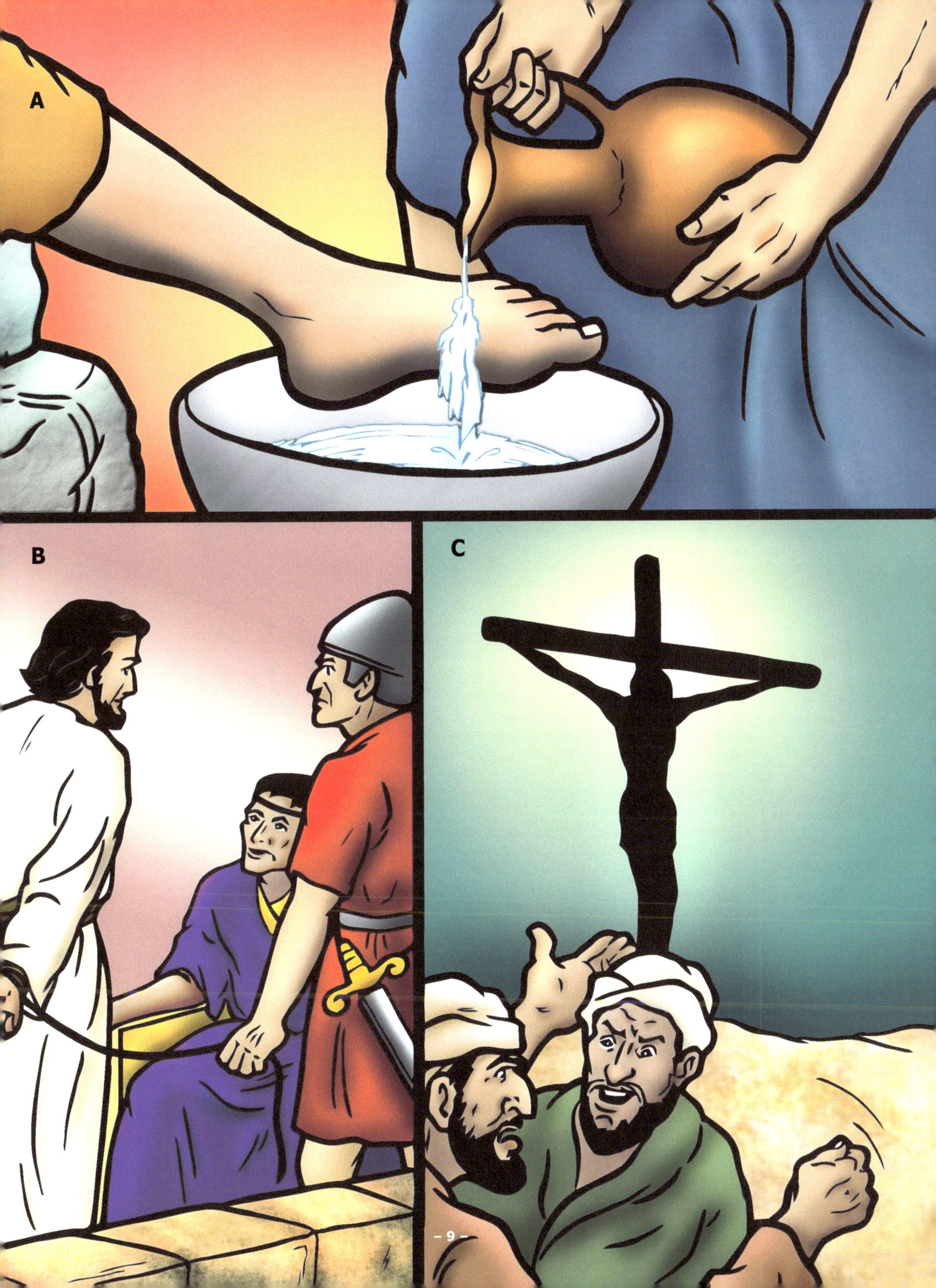

For we are His workmanship, created in Christ Jesus unto good works.

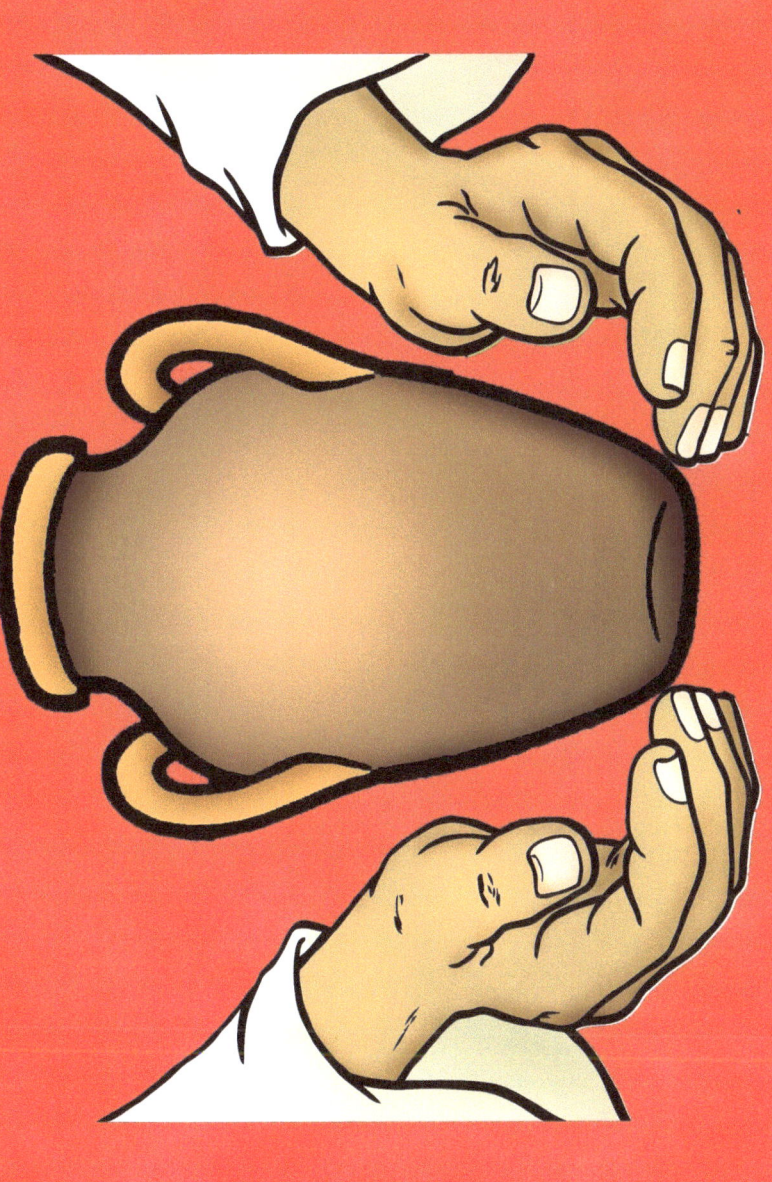

Ephesians 2:10a

© Bible Visuals International Inc

Lesson 1
THE BELIEVERS CHOSEN AND ADOPTED

> **NOTE TO THE TEACHER**
>
> When Paul wrote to the churches, he first instructed them in doctrine. Then he taught them how to put the doctrine into practice. In the book of Ephesians he follows the same pattern. He reveals the high position of believers: they are in Christ (chapters 1-3).
>
> Then he unfolds how the believer who is so richly blessed should behave (chapters 4-6). The privileges and responsibilities of the believer in Christ are made known.
>
> God never makes mistakes. He has chosen believers and planned for them to be holy and without blame before Him. This does not mean that God has chosen some people to be lost. He has never said this. (See 2 Peter 3:9; compare Ezekiel 33:11.) He invites all to come to Him.
>
> In teaching the truth of adoption, make it perfectly clear that God has placed us as sons in His family, declaring us to be far more than servants.

Scripture to be studied: Ephesians 1:1-5; all verses in the text.

The *aim* of the lesson: To show that God has chosen all who are believers and has chosen them to be holy and without blame. In His love, He has adopted each believer as His son and heir.

What your students should *know*: It is because of Christ's death that believers are chosen and adopted.

What your students should *feel*: The awe of being chosen by God before the foundation of the world; the joy of being His sons and heirs.

What your students should *do*:

Saved: Share the truths of being chosen and adopted with a Christian who has not had this lesson.

Unsaved: Turn to the One who says "Whosoever will may come," receiving Him as Saviour and Lord.

Lesson outline (for the teacher's and students' notebooks):
1. Believers are in Christ (Ephesians 1:3).
2. Believers were chosen before the world was made (Ephesians 1:4).
   A. Chosen to be in Christ
   B. Chosen to be holy and without blame
3. Believers are adopted (Ephesians 1:5).
   A. Adopted because of Jesus Christ
   B. Adopted as sons and heirs of God

The verse to be memorized:

For we are His workmanship, created in Christ Jesus unto good works . . . (Ephesians 2:10a)

THE LESSON

A secret is fun, especially if you are one who knows what the secret is. The book of Ephesians, which we begin to study today, is filled with secrets for the person who believes in Christ. You will enjoy discovering what these secrets are.

1. BELIEVERS ARE IN CHRIST
Ephesians 1:3

Thirteen or 14 of our New Testament books were written by the Apostle Paul. He wrote the letter to the Ephesian church while he was in prison in Rome. He could hardly wait to tell the Christians the first secret. Immediately after his greeting he writes that God has given believers every spiritual good thing right here on earth. We don't have to wait to have good things in Heaven. We have them in this life because of what the Lord Jesus has done for us.

Before the coming of Christ, God blessed His people, the Jews, with earthly good things: long life, wealth, success. (See Exodus 20:12; Joshua 1:8.) They enjoyed these blessings here on earth. Since Christ Jesus came, God blesses Christians with heavenly good things: forgiveness of sins, peace with God, true happiness, and much more. Although these are heavenly things, we enjoy them here and now on earth. It is so because of this important fact: believers are in Christ. (See Ephesians 1:3b.)

We Christians speak of having Christ in us. This is true. (See Colossians 1:27.) He does live within us. But it is equally true that we are in Him. (See, for example, Ephesians 2:5-6.) It is because we are in Christ that we are heavenly people. So we have heavenly treasures.

Please write in your notebook this first secret revealed in Ephesians:

1. Believers are in Christ, and ARE blessed with ALL heavenly good things (Ephesians 1:3).

2. BELIEVERS WERE CHOSEN BEFORE THE WORLD WAS MADE
Ephesians 1:4

Secret number two follows quickly in Ephesians. Before we look at it, let me tell you a story. There was a farmer whom we shall call Mr. Edwards. Mr. Edwards announced at an orphanage that he wanted someone to help him on his farm. On Thursday he would see any who were interested. You could not guess how many boys and girls crowded into the room on Thursday. Mr. Edwards began, "I have work for each one of you. The work is not easy. I will need you 24 hours a day, seven days a week."

Some of the children grumbled. Others left the room.

Mr. Edwards continued, "I promise you that if you work for me, you will be glad. I will want you to do things the way I show you. This may seem hard at first."

More children complained and left. Mr. Edwards could hardly be heard above the commotion. "If you work with me, I'll make certain you have an opportunity for an education."

One boy rudely exclaimed, "Why don't you talk about money?" He rushed out of the room leading many others. Few were left after this.

"I knew most would not stay," Mr. Edwards said. "But I knew that those who really wanted to work would stay. If you are willing to do as I say, come to me one by one and sign here." A few of the remaining ones signed.

"I have had my eye on each of you for some time," Mr. Edwards said. "You are the ones I knew would join me. I had enough work for all who were here. But I planned to keep only those who would work with me in my way.

"Since you have signed, I have many things to share with you. You will receive an education while you are working with me. I have chosen you to be my own children. This home will always be yours."

– 18 –

"We're chosen!" one of the boys shouted. "Chosen by Mr. Edwards to share his home. We're chosen!"

2A. CHOSEN TO BE IN CHRIST

Chosen. That is secret number two.

Show Illustration #1a

Even before the world was made, God chose believers to be in Christ. (See Ephesians 1:4.)

Show Illustration #1b

Before the world was made, God knew that He would give His Son to die for you. (See Acts 2:23.) God chose you and Christ died for you. If you have received Him, you are His forever.

Perhaps you want to know how to be absolutely certain that God chose you. You're thinking of the kind of life you lived before you became a Christian. You wonder why God would choose a sinner like you.

Show Illustration #1c

(*Teacher*: Over the door print the words:)
**THE WAY TO LIFE
WHOSOEVER WILL**

God saw you as He sees each person on the road of life. To each one He says, "Whosoever will may come through the door that leads to everlasting life." (See John 3:16; 14:6; Revelation 3:20; 22:17.) The day God spoke to you, you answered, "I believe that the Lord Jesus Christ is the Son of God. I will accept His invitation." Though others turned away, you entered the door.

Show Illustration #1d

(*Teacher*: On the cross print the words:)
CHOSEN IN CHRIST

After receiving the Lord Jesus Christ, you turned to look at the door through which you had come. Inside were the words: *Chosen in Christ Before the World was Made.* (See 2 Thessalonians 2:13; 1 Peter 1:2.)

You could have turned from the love of God, refusing to enter the door, as others have done. If you had, you would be separated from God forever. You yourself would be responsible. Even though God chose you for Himself before He made the world, you had to put your trust in the Lord Jesus Christ in order to be saved.

Believers are chosen in Christ. This is part of the second secret of Ephesians. But there is more.

2B. CHOSEN TO BE HOLY AND WITHOUT BLAME

Show Illustration #2

Not only did God choose to save you, He chose to make you holy and without blame. (See Ephesians 1:4b; Jude 24, 25.) We studied this word *holy* when we studied the book of Romans. It is exactly the same word as *sanctify*. It means to be set apart by God for Himself. He sets you apart to make you like Christ. (See Romans 8:29.) You are set apart for Him now in this life. You will be His set-apart-one all through eternity. When you stand before Him, you will be without blame for your sin. All of this is possible because Christ died for you.

This is the second secret for your notebook:

2. God chose believers. He chose them to be in Christ and to be holy and without blame.

3. BELIEVERS ARE ADOPTED
Ephesians 1:5

Before we have the third secret of the book of Ephesians, think again of the story we had earlier about Mr. Edwards and the orphans. Suppose a day came when Mr. Edwards said, "I have shared my home with you. Now I want to do more. I am going to adopt you as my own sons and daughters. My name will be your name. Not only will I share my home with you, but I will now share all I have. Everything will be yours."

3A. ADOPTED BECAUSE OF JESUS CHRIST

Part of the third secret is: God adopts believers as His own sons (Ephesians 1:5; see also John 1:12; Romans 8:15; Galatians 4:5).

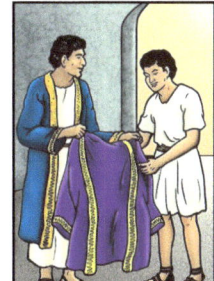
Show Illustration #3

In our study of Galatians we learned that in the time of Paul there was a custom of declaring grown boys as sons. At a certain age a ceremony was held in which the boy received a coat like his father's. Then the boy was placed as a son in the family. This son placing was known as adoption. Before adoption, even though the boy was his father's child, he was not much more than a servant. (See Galatians 4:1.) After adoption, he was honored as his father's son. He no doubt continued his father's work. He shared his father's riches.

The moment you received the Lord Jesus Christ as Saviour, you became a child of God. You were born again, and this new birth brought you into the family of God. You were a Christian, one belonging to Christ. That in itself is a wonderful truth. The secret of Ephesians is that, in addition, God immediately "adopted" you and made you His son. (See Galatians 3:26, where the correct word is *sons*.) Because you are a son, He corrects you when it is necessary. (See Hebrews 12:5-11.)

You are not only God's child. You are His son.

3B. ADOPTED AS SONS AND HEIRS OF GOD

Show Illustration #4a

In Paul's day, the adopted son became his father's heir. That meant that one day the son received everything that belonged to his father: lands, cattle, sheep, home, jewels, money, everything.

Before God made the world, He determined that when you received Christ as Saviour you would be His son. Because you are His son, he now provides your needs each day.

Show Illustration #4b

When the Lord Jesus comes for His own, you and each son of God will share His riches forever and forever. (See Romans 8:17; 1 Corinthians 3:22-23; 1 John 3:2; 1 Thessalonians 4:14-17.)

This third secret should be written in your notebook:

3. Believers are adopted as God's sons and heirs (Ephesians 1:5).

Perhaps you've never before realized that you were chosen by God before the foundation of the world. You never knew that He adopted you as His son and heir. Maybe you'd like to lead in prayer right now thanking the Lord for this high position that you have in Christ. (*Teacher:* Allow students time to pray.)

There are Christians in this town who do not know these wonderful secrets from Ephesians. They do not know that they are in Christ and blessed now with all heavenly good things. They have not understood that God chose them before the foundation of the world chose them to be holy and without blame before Him. They have no idea that they are adopted by God, having the honor of being placed as His sons and heirs.

Write in your notebook the name of a Christian friend with whom you would like to share these truths this week. Now we shall pray that God will help you to make these secrets clear.

Lesson 2
THE BELIEVERS—ACCEPTED, REDEEMED, SEALED

NOTE TO THE TEACHER

The greatest revelation which is given in the Ephesian Epistle is that God has redeemed believing sinners by the blood of His Son and exalted them in Christ to the highest possible position. The creation of the world is a masterpiece of God. His redemption of sinners is an even greater masterpiece. This is why we have chosen Ephesians 2:10 as our memory verse. We are His workmanship, His masterpiece.

Your students will grow spiritually and their Christian joy will be increased as they study the truths of Ephesians.

Take time to make each truth perfectly clear, perhaps presenting only one new fact in a lesson. Let the students discuss the facts until they feel the wonder of each one.

Remember: Every spiritual blessing is ours because Christ died and rose again for us. Can we do less than give Him everything we have?

Give your pupils opportunity to tell their experiences in sharing with others the first three Ephesian "secrets."

Scripture to be studied: Ephesians 1:6-14; all verses in the text.

The *aim* of the lesson: To show that every person who truly receives Christ as personal Saviour is accepted, redeemed, and sealed forever.

What your students should *know*: All of these glorious facts are true because the believer is in Christ.

What your students should *feel*: An overwhelming desire to live for the One who has done all this for them.

What your students should *do*:
Saved: Share these truths with one other Christian this week.
Unsaved: Receive the Saviour at once.

Lesson outline (for the teacher's and students notebooks):
1. Believers are in Christ (Ephesians 1:3, 4, 6, 7, 10-11).
2. Believers are accepted by God (1:6).
3. Believers are redeemed by Christ (1:7).
4. Believers are sealed by the Holy Spirit (1:13).

The verse to be memorized:

We are His workmanship, created in Christ Jesus unto good works . . . (Ephesians 2:10a)

THE LESSON

Some years ago on a small island in the Philippines, the Taal Volcano erupted. Boiling lava shot into the sky. When it fell on the island below, it destroyed everything on which it settled: animals, houses, people. Some families who lived close to the shore hastily loaded their cows, sewing machines, grain, and whatever they could grab, onto little boats and escaped safely. They were saved because they were in boats.

1. BELIEVERS ARE IN CHRIST
Ephesians 1:3-4, 6-7, 10-11

Show Illustration #5

Far more wonderful than being safe in boats, is to be safe in Christ. The truth of being in Christ is repeated often in the first chapter of Ephesians. (You may want to mark the expressions. "in Christ," "in whom," "in Him," which appear in verses 3-4, 6-7, 10-11.) It is because we are in Christ that we have all heavenly good things. For example, we are chosen in Him (verse 4), as we studied in our last lesson. Today we will learn that we are accepted in Him (verse 6); and we have redemption in Him (verse 7). We have life–eternal life–in Him (John 1:4). These heavenly things and all others are ours now because we are in Christ. (See Ephesians 1:3.)

We may have many good earthly things. (*Teacher*: name "good things" which your students treasure.) Or we may have only a few good things. As Christians, we can be satisfied with or without good earthly things because we have every good heavenly thing. Our earthly things may be destroyed. The good heavenly things are ours now and forever. Because we are in Christ, God keeps us safe in His almighty hand forever. (See John 10:28-29; 1 Corinthians 3:22-23.)

That was the first secret we found in the book of Ephesians: We have every heavenly good thing because we are in Christ. The other secrets are: (2) We were chosen in Christ before the world was made, chosen to be made holy and without blame before Him. (3) We are elevated to the privileged position of being His sons and heirs. Today we learn secrets four, five and six.

2. BELIEVERS ARE ACCEPTED BY GOD
Ephesians 1:6

The fourth secret is this: Because of God's grace. we are *accepted* in Christ, the Beloved (Ephesians 1:6).

God's grace is His kindness and His loving favor given to those who should have His punishment. You cannot earn His grace. You cannot earn His loving-kindness. He gives it to you because of His love.

Many years ago in England a woman planned to stab the queen to death. She hid in a closet, not realizing that the rooms would be searched before the queen went to bed. She was found, dragged before the queen, and her dagger was wrenched from her. Realizing her helplessness, she fell before the queen crying for pity. "Be gracious," she begged.

The queen responded, "I pardon you out of my grace." So the woman was led away free. She deserved punishment. She received grace.

Show Illustration #6

God's grace is far greater than the queen's grace. Not only does He love you, but He loves you just as He loves His Son. (See John 17:23.) Think of that! God has accepted you because you are in Christ.

If you have placed your trust in the Saviour, you can say, "God has accepted me in Christ." You are His very own. (See John 17:9-10.)

Please write this fourth secret in your notebook:

4. God has accepted believers in Christ.

Now for secret number five in Ephesians.

3. BELIEVERS ARE REDEEMED BY CHRIST
Ephesians 1:7

We read, "In whom we have redemp-tion through His blood" (Ephesians 1:7). Here is another heavenly good thing that you have in Christ: redemption. If you are a child of God, you have been redeemed.

Show Illustration #7a

Redeem is an important Bible word. It means to buy by paying a price. A slave is brought into the market to be sold. Someone pays money for him. Now that slave belongs to the one who bought him. Before you were saved, you were a slave of sin. You could do nothing to get yourself free. So the Lord Jesus bought you by paying a price for you. He redeemed you.

The word *redeem* includes another thought: to buy out of the market. That is, the one who has been purchased will never be put on sale again. He will always belong to the one who bought him. When the Lord Jesus paid for you, He not only bought you but He bought you to be His forever. (See Hebrews 9:12.)

Show Illustration #7b

There is still more included in the word *redeem*. It means to loose or set free by paying a price. The person who paid for the slave freed him from his former owner. Like the slave, you, too have been freed if you have received the Lord Jesus as your Saviour. (See Romans 8:2.) You have been freed from the punishment you deserved for your sins. You are freed from all blame forever.

You were bought. Did you notice what it was that paid for your redemption? It was not money, nor silver or gold. You were bought, redeemed with the precious blood of the Lord Jesus Christ. (See 1 Peter 1:18, 19, Ephesians 1:7; Revelation 5:9.) Because this is so, your sins are forgiven. (See Ephesians 1:7.) You are as clear before God as if you had never sinned. This means that absolutely every sin has been paid for by Christ's blood. He has redeemed you from the sins you committed before you were saved, those which you have done since you were saved, and whatever sins you may do the rest of your life.

The sins you have done since you were born again and the sins you will yet do, cannot cut you off from God. You are His forever because you are in Christ. However, sinning does break your friendship with Him. To renew that friendship, you must confess your sins. (See 1 John 1:9.)

It is because you are a redeemed one that God lets you know these and other secrets of His. (See Ephesians 1:9.) He wants you to remember these things.

So will you please write the fifth secret in your notebook:

5. Believers are redeemed by the precious blood of Christ.
    a. They are bought.
    b. They belong forever to the One who bought them.
    c. They are free from all punishment forever.

If you are in Christ, you are accepted by God the Father. You are redeemed by Christ the Son. Now get ready for the sixth secret.

4. SEALED BY THE HOLY SPIRIT
Ephesians 1:13

When you heard the Gospel, you placed your trust in Christ. When you trusted in Him, you were sealed immediately with the Holy Spirit of God. (Read that, please, in Ephesians 1:13.) (*Teacher:* In English the two phrases beginning with the word *after* are sometimes confusing. The original thought is that when they heard, or upon hearing the Gospel, they trusted in Christ. And when they believed, or upon believing in Him, they were sealed with the Holy Spirit.)

In Bible times, a seal was a mark of ownership. That mark let others know who owned the person or thing that was sealed. It was also a mark of approval. It let everyone know that the owner approved that which was sealed.

The Bible tells us that God the Father sealed God the Son. (See John 6:27.) He was sealed with the Holy Spirit at the time He was baptized. (See Matthew 3:17.) The Spirit of God, like a dove, came down on Him, and God spoke from heaven saying, "This is My beloved Son." God let the people know that the Lord Jesus was His. "This is My beloved Son in whom I am well pleased." This was His announcement that He approved the Lord Jesus. He sealed Him.

Show Illustration #8

When you believed in the Lord Jesus and trusted Him as your Saviour, the same blessed Holy Spirit came to live in you. (The Holy Spirit cannot be seen, for He is a spirit. We have pictured a dove to remind us that He came upon the Lord Jesus as a dove.) The Holy Spirit sealed you. It is as if God said, "This person belongs to Me. I approve him."

That is secret number six for your notebook:

6. Believers are sealed by the Holy Spirit.

Although Paul wrote many epistles, he mentioned the sealing of the Spirit in only two: Ephesians and Second Corinthians (1:22). That is because the people in Ephesus and Corinth would have understood the meaning of a seal. Those two cities were centers of the lumber industry. A raft of logs would be brought to the harbor, and men would look them over. One would say, "I will take these logs." Another, "I will take those." Each would pay a little money (called "earnest money"), which was a promise that later he would pay the rest that he owed. At the same time he made a certain mark on each log, using a mark that was his alone. This was his seal. Sometime afterwards each lumberman paid the rest of the money and got his logs. He knew his own logs by the seal.

The Lord knows those who are His (see John 10:14; 2 Timothy 2:19) because each is sealed by the Holy Spirit. When He sealed you it was His earnest, His promise, that He will some day present you to God. (See Ephesians 1:14.) There in heaven, you and every redeemed one will add to God's glory forever. Think of that!

These are the six secrets from the first part of Ephesians:

1. Believers are in Christ and, therefore, have every heavenly good thing.
2. God chose believers before the world was made.
3. God "adopted" believers as His sons and heirs.
4. God accepted believers.
5. Believers have been redeemed by the Lord Jesus.
6. The Holy Spirit seals believers.

Think of one Christian with whom you can share these truths. Write that person's name in your notebook right now. Then we shall pray that God will give you the opportunity this week to show him these wonderful facts from Ephesians.

If you have never received the Lord Jesus, He is waiting for you to turn to Him (*Teacher*: Point to cross on Illustration #7.) He loves you so much that He died for you. He proved that He is the Son of God by rising from the dead.

The moment you place your trust in Him, each of these tremendous realities will be true of you. Will you receive Him as your Saviour right now?

Lesson 3
LIVING THE LIFE OF THE BELIEVER

NOTE TO THE TEACHER

The first three chapters of Ephesians reveal our high position in Christ. The last three chapters (4-6) teach us that our high position in Christ should affect our daily living.

Seven times in this epistle the Apostle Paul uses the word *walk* to show the life history of any Christian: See 2:2; 2:10; 4:l; 4:17; 5:2; 5:8; 5:15. In view of the fact that we are redeemed by the precious blood of Christ, our behavior is to be ordered of God. We are to walk worthy of our high calling. All that God says we are, should be evidenced in our daily lives.

Scripture to be studied: Ephesians 4:1–6:9

The *aim* of the lesson: To show that God wants each believer to live like Christ when he is with other believers, when he is with unbelievers, and when he is with his family.

What your students should *know*: That God expects them to walk worthy of all that they are in Christ.

What your students should *feel*: A keen desire to have their earthly lives match their heavenly position in Christ.

What your students should *do*:

Saved: Decide upon a particular situation (with unbelievers, believers, or in the family) in which they will "walk worthy of the Lord" this week.

Unsaved: Receive the Lord Jesus as Saviour.

Lesson outline (for the teacher's and students' notebooks):

1. The believer is to behave to please God (Ephesians 4:1-2).
2. Believers and unbelievers (Ephesians 4:17-24; 5:1-20).
3. Believers and other believers (Ephesians 4:25-32).
4. Believers and their families (Ephesians 5:21; 6:9).

The verse to be memorized:

For we are His workmanship, created in Christ Jesus unto good works . . . (Ephesians 2:10a)

THE LESSON

When you were learning to walk, you had to think about every step you took. That is not true now. You never have to say to yourself, "I will put my right foot forward; now my left." When you come to a mud puddle, you do not say, "Feet, jump over that puddle." You jump over it so simply that later you would not remember there had been a puddle in your path.

In the Ephesian letter, Paul shows that living the Christian life is like walking. He says we are to walk (live) worthy of all that we are. In the first chapter he reveals six tremendous truths about us who have received Christ as our Saviour. We are in Christ; God has chosen us, "adopted" us, accepted us; Christ has redeemed us; and the Holy Spirit has sealed us. Since all of these heavenly good things are true of us, we are to live the kind of life that matches them. This may not be any easier than when we first learned to walk physically. It means we will have to learn a completely new kind of behavior. In the last three chapters of Ephesians we are taught how to walk worthy of Christ, what kind of life we should live and among whom we are to live it.

1. THE BELIEVER'S BEHAVIOR
Ephesians 4:1-2

God says we are to live "with all lowliness and meekness, with longsuffering, forbearing one another in love" (Ephesians 4:2).

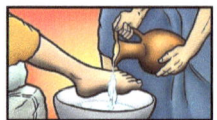

Show Illustration #9a

While the Lord Jesus was on earth, He lived with "all lowliness." That is, He did things without showing off. Shortly before His death, He washed His disciples' feet. (See John 13:2-17; compare Philippians 2:3.) The disciples should have washed His feet, for He is the Lord. Instead, like a servant, He washed their feet, saying, "I have given you an example, that you should do as I have done to you." (See John 13:15.) Like Him, we are to do things for others without showing off.

Once the Lord Jesus spoke of Himself as "lowly in heart." At the same time He said, "I am meek." (See Matthew 11:29; compare 2 Corinthians 10:1.)

Show Illustration #9b

The Lord Jesus was tried unfairly by Pilate. People accused Him of things that were not true. However, He stood meekly, not answering a word. (See Matthew 27:12-14; 1 Peter 2:23; Isaiah 53:7.) We, too, are to practice meekness. This means we are not to get angry when people are unkind to us.

Show Illustration #9c

Along with being lowly and meek, we are to be longsuffering (patient). The people who crucified the Lord Jesus sneered at Him, saying and doing evil things to Him. For these very people He prayed, "Father, forgive them, for they do not know what they are doing." (See Luke 23:34.) Like Him, we are not to be bad tempered when things go against us or when people do wrong to us.

We are to put up with one another lovingly ("forbearing one another in love"). We are also to be at peace with one another. Why? Because each believer is a part of the Body of Christ and indwelt by the Holy Spirit (Ephesians 4:3). So, like the parts of our physical bodies, we must cooperate with other believers in building up the Body of Christ. (See Ephesians 4:13, 16.)

By not showing off, by not getting angry at people who are unkind to us, by not being bad-tempered, by putting up with others lovingly, and by living peacefully with others, we walk worthy of Christ. This may not be any easier than for children learning to walk. Our old sin natures are the opposite of lowly, meek, longsuffering, loving. Unfortunately, our old natures are with us all our lives. So we often do what we should not do. And God holds us responsible for those wrongs because we should be allowing the Holy Spirit to control us. The believer's behavior should be pleasing to God.

2. BELIEVERS AND UNBELIEVERS
Ephesians 4:17-24; 5:1-20

Believers are always to walk worthy of Christ even when they are among unbelievers.

Long before the time of Paul a little girl whose home was in Israel was taken as a slave to Syria. We do not know her real name so suppose we call her Adah. Adah became the servant girl for the wife of Naaman—a general in the Syrian army. Adah loved the true and living God of heaven. Because she belonged to Him, she did her work well.

One day a great sadness came into the general's home. Naaman had leprosy. In those days, that was a disease for which there was no cure.

Adah remembered a man of God, Elisha, who lived in her homeland. The Lord had used him to do miracles. Adah felt certain that Elisha could heal Naaman of his leprosy. She decided to tell Mrs. Naaman about God and about Elisha.

Then a terrifying thought popped into Adah's head: *I am only a slave. These are important people. They probably will not listen to me. I better keep still about God.* Immediately Adah knew that thought was wrong. So she simply asked the Lord to give her courage to speak of Him.

Show Illustration #10a

God answered her prayer for she said to Mrs. Naaman, "I wish the general would go to my country. There is a man of God there who could heal him." She, a slave, made a suggestion to the wife of the general! The word got to Naaman. Apparently he knew that Adah was a good slave who always told the truth. Consequently, Naaman accepted her suggestion. He went to God's man, Elisha. He did what Elisha told him to do, and God healed him. (See 2 Kings 5:1-19.) Naaman turned to God because Adah had lived for Him.

Perhaps you are wondering how it is possible to walk worthy of Christ among unbelievers. The secret is to "be renewed in the spirit of your mind" (Ephesians 4:23). Your physical body is renewed by eating food.

Show Illustration #10b

Your spirit and your mind are renewed by the Word of God. (See Job 23:12.) By studying it, you will know how God wants you to live. From the Bible you will receive strength for doing what God wants you to do.

3. BELIEVERS AND OTHER BELIEVERS
Ephesians 4:25-32

We are to walk worthy of the Lord Jesus Christ when we are with unbelievers. We are also to walk worthy of Him when we are with believers. Sometimes Christians forget this. Even the Ephesians must have forgotten it, for Paul says: "Stop lying. Speak the truth, for we belong to each other. Do not be angry. Do not give the devil a foothold. Do not steal. Work with your hands. Do not use bad language. Say that which is good so that others will be helped." (See Ephesians 4:25-29.)

Have you ever lied to another Christian? Did you ever get angry with another Christian? Have you ever taken something from another believer? What about using bad language when speaking to someone who loves the Lord? If you have done any of these things, you have grieved the Holy Spirit who lives inside you. (See Ephesians 4:30.)

When you received the Lord Jesus Christ as your Savior, the Holy Spirit came to live in your heart. (We use the dove to remind us that He came like a dove upon the Lord Jesus. But because He is a spirit, we cannot see Him.) He sealed you, marking you as God's child forever. He never leaves you. (See John 14:16.) So when you disobey the Word of God, He is grieved. This is a serious thing.

Show Illustration #11a

When He is grieved, you are not happy inside. You do not enjoy reading the Bible or praying. You find it hard to tell others about the Lord Jesus. Grieving the Holy Spirit is sin.

Show Illustration #11b

Sin must be confessed to God. You must tell Him what you have done wrong and ask Him to forgive you. (See 1 John 1:9.)

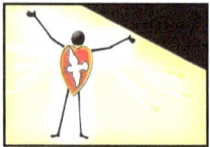

Show Illustration #11c

When you have received His forgiveness, you are to forgive others, as He has forgiven you. (See Ephesians 4:32.)

4. BELIEVERS AND THEIR FAMILIES
Ephesians 5:21–6:9

Since we are in Christ, we are to walk worthy of Him, both when we are with unbelievers and with believers. We are also to walk worthy of Him in our homes. In some ways, this may be the hardest place to live like the Lord Jesus.

In the two closing chapters of Ephesians, there are instructions for each one in the home: husbands, wives, children, servants, masters. (*Teacher:* Read to your class the verses that have to do with your particular group.)

Christian husbands are to be in charge of the family, just as Christ is the Head of the church. The husband works so that he can take care of the needs of the family. By doing so, he is an example of the care which the Lord takes of His own. Fathers are to be willing to give everything they have for their families, just as Christ gave His life for us. Wives are to submit to their husbands just as they would obey the Lord. (See 1 Peter 3:1.) Children are to obey and honor their parents because "this is right." It pleases the Lord. (See Colossians 3:20.)

Being disobedient to parents is one thing about which God's Word speaks most sternly. The Bible says that this is one of the worst sins. (See Romans 1:29-30.) Children, if you are born again, you are to show it at home by obeying your parents.

Mary and Joseph loved the child Jesus. They cared for Him, even though they did not always understand Him. When He was 12 years old, they took Him to Jerusalem for the Passover Feast. Afterwards Mary and Joseph started home along with many others. They traveled a whole day, supposing Jesus was with them. But He was not. So they went back to Jerusalem and, after three days of searching, they found Him. He was sitting in the house of God, talking with the teachers.

Mary said, "We have had much sorrow looking for You."

Jesus answered, "Why were you looking all over Jerusalem for Me? Did you not realize that I would be in My Father's house?"

Show Illustration #12

Although God was His Father, Jesus went home with Mary and Joseph and was obedient to them. He, the Creator of all, obeyed His earthly parents. What an example He is to us!

Those in the family who work, are to work as if they were serving the Lord Himself. Those who are bosses are to treat those who work for them as they want their Father in Heaven to treat them.

You may be with unbelievers and believers this week. You will be in your home. Suppose you suggest some things which Christians can do to walk worthy of the Lord. (*Teacher*: Allow the class to discuss what believers could do when they are with unbelievers, believers, and in the home. Review the illustrations in the lesson to give them ideas.) Think of one circumstance in which you can walk worthy of the Lord this week. Write that in your notebook. Then we shall pray together that God will help you to live as Christ would have you live.

Lesson 4
THE BELIEVER AND THE ENEMY

NOTE TO THE TEACHER

As soon as the apostle finishes his admonition to the members of Christian families, he turns to the subject of the Christian's warfare. We go from the home to the battlefield to meet cruel enemies. Those enemies try to destroy our Christian experience. They tempt us to do or say things that will bring dishonor to the name of our blessed Lord. We are reminded that although we have every heavenly good thing, we are still very much in the world. As long as we are here, we will be in conflict with the evil one.

Give your students opportunity to tell what they did to walk worthy of the Lord since the last lesson.

Scripture to be studied: Ephesians 6:10-20

The *aim* of the lesson: To show that only those who are in Christ can defeat the devil.

What your students should *know*: The believer's daily warfare is as real as Satan himself.

What your students should *feel*: A desire to live a life of victory.

What your students should *do*:
Saved: Yield themselves completely to Christ who is able to win every victory over the evil one.
Unsaved: Accept the Saviour so they will not spend eternity with the devil and his angels.

Lesson outline (for the teacher's and students' notebooks):
1. The believer's power (Ephesians 6:10).
2. The believer's enemy (Ephesians 6:12).
3. The believer's armor (Ephesians 6:13-18).
4. The believer's Victor.

The verse to be memorized:

For we are His workmanship, created in Christ Jesus unto good works . . . (Ephesians 2:10a)

THE LESSON

Did you know that you are a soldier in a war? You are, and you will have one battle after another all the days of your life. (See 2 Corinthians 10:3-5.) Think of that!

Our memory verse reminds us that we who are Christians are God's workmanship. The stars, the moon, the sun, trees and flowers–all are the workmanship of God. But if you are a Christian, you are not only His workmanship, you are His masterpiece! He has given you every heavenly good thing: you are in Christ, God has chosen you, "adopted" you, accepted you; the Lord Jesus has redeemed you; the Holy Spirit has sealed you. He has created you in Christ Jesus unto good works. That is, you are to live as Christ would live with unbelievers and believers. Especially are you to live like Him in your home.

Because the Lord Jesus is the exact opposite of your old sinful nature, it will be a battle to live as He would have you live.

1. THE BELIEVER'S POWER
Ephesians 6:10

That is why the apostle tells us near the end of Ephesians that we are to be strong in the Lord. You are in Christ, and Christ is in you. He is the One who gives you the power to live the Christian life. You are created in Him to do good works.

2. THE BELIEVER'S ENEMY
Ephesians 6:12

You need to be strong in your daily life because you have a powerful enemy, Satan. Satan and his evil spirits hate God; they hate our blessed Saviour. They hate you! So they seek to bring dishonor to the Lord by leading you to do wrong things–things that grieve the Holy Spirit.

You are not fighting against people. You are in battle against evil beings whom you cannot see. Their purpose is to control people. They strive to hinder men and women and boys and girls from believing the truth of God. Satan and his host do their very best to keep you from honoring the Lord Jesus. They aim to keep you from prayer, from Bible study, and from the joy God wants you to have.

3. THE BELIEVER'S ARMOR
Ephesians 6:13-18

In order to win the battle against Satan and his forces, we are told to take to ourselves immediately the complete armor of God. That armor includes a belt, a breastplate, shoes, a shield, a helmet, and a sword. These are all that you need, but you need them *all* to protect you from your enemy. Listen closely now, and get ready for a surprise.

Show Illustration #13

"Stand therefore, having your loins girt about with truth." The Ephesians who wore long flowing garments understood this perfectly. When a man was fighting, he wanted to keep his robe out of the way. So he drew it up around his waist and held it in place with a wide, strong belt. This belt was worn about the loins, the place of strength. When you lift heavy things, you get your strength from your loins. As a Christian you must have protection for this place of strength. And it is the belt of truth that guards your strength. A truthful Christian is a strong soldier. A Christian who does not tell the truth will lose every battle against Satan and his army.

Along with the belt of truth, you are to have "the breastplate of righteousness." The breastplate covers the soldier's heart. Everyone knows that the enemy's target is the heart. If the soldier's heart is hit, the soldier is finished. It is your heart, Christian, that causes you to do right or wrong. (See Proverbs 23:7a; Mark 7:20-23.) The covering for the heart is righteousness or right doing. Doing right includes doing good things without showing off. You do right when you are not bad-tempered or do not get angry when people do wrong to you. When you put up with others lovingly and are at peace with them, you do right. Every day you are to have on the belt of truth and the breastplate of righteousness.

Show Illustration #14

As a Christian soldier you must have your "feet shod with the preparation of the Gospel of peace." (See Isaiah 52:7.) These shoes protect your feet when you take the Good News of peace to unbelievers wherever they are. You walk worthy of Christ when you have the Gospel shoes on.

Over all, you are to take "the shield of faith, wherewith you shall be able to quench all the fiery darts of the wicked." When you trust in God instead of yourself, you have the shield of faith. It is this shield that protects you from Satan's fiery darts. Fiery darts set clothes on fire and cause wounded soldiers to burn to death in awful pain. The devil loves to see you suffer after he hits you. You will suffer when you cannot witness because you failed to live like a Christian, or if you disobeyed your parents. Use your shield of faith to protect you from Satan.

Now, Christian soldier, place a helmet on your head to protect it. It is with your head, your mind, that you think. You know you are saved, but you are to understand your salvation. By studying Ephesians you know that God has chosen you, adopted you, and accepted you. You know that Christ has redeemed you, and the Holy Spirit has sealed you. All of this and more is included in your salvation. Think about these things so your mind is protected from evil thoughts.

Show Illustration #15

The belt, the breastplate, the shoes, the shield, and the helmet protect you from the enemy. But you must have "the sword of the Spirit which is the Word of God" so that you can go out to attack the enemy. Having the sword (the Word of God) is not enough. You must know how to use it. If you know what the Bible says, you can quote it to Satan. That is exactly what the Lord Jesus did when Satan tried to get Him to do wrong. (See Matthew 4:1-11.) Suppose, for example, the devil tempts you to buy something for yourself when you know in your heart you should give that money to God. You should say to Satan, "God's Word says, 'Seek ye first the kingdom of God, and His righteousness; and all these things shall be added unto you' " (Matthew 6:33). When you give that money to God, you send the devil running.

You are to use your armor with prayer: "Praying always with all prayer." Bible study and prayer go together. Without them, you will be a defeated soldier.

4. THE BELIEVER'S VICTORY

Now here is a surprising thing about the Christian's armor. It is not simply some things. It is a Person! Listen closely. (*Teacher:* See Romans 13:12, 14.)

We have the strong belt of truth. It was the Lord Jesus who said, "I am the way, the truth." (See John 14:6.) He who is the Truth keeps us strong by making us truthful.

Next is the breastplate of righteousness, or right doing. The Lord Jesus Christ is the Righteous One. (See Jeremiah 23:6; 1 John 2:1; 1 Corinthians 1:30.) Because He lives in your heart, He Himself will protect your heart.

The Good News of Peace shoes are next. In Ephesians we learn that Christ is our peace. (See Ephesians 2:14.) No wonder we do not have to be afraid in the daily Christian battle. The Prince of Peace is always with us.

Our shield of faith is the Lord Jesus. (See Genesis 15:1.) He who has never lost a battle will stop Satan's fiery darts, for He is our shield of faith. (See Galatians 2:20.)

By now you have guessed that the helmet of salvation is also the Lord Jesus. He is there always to protect our minds. (See Psalm 27:1.)

The Sword of the Spirit is the Word of God. The Bible is the written Word. The Lord Jesus in the incarnate Word. (See John 1:1-14.) Every day, every moment, no matter where you are, your whole armor is the Lord Jesus Christ Himself.

Show Illustration #16

You are in Christ. If you obey Him, you can be certain that He will cause you to win each battle against Satan and his wicked angels. The One who defeated Satan when He arose from the dead wants to give you victory today. (See Romans 8:37.)

Will you promise to be a good soldier for Jesus Christ? When Satan comes after you today, will you be prepared to meet him? You will be if you yield yourself to the Lord Jesus. Will you do that right now?

(*Teacher:* Encourage your students to discuss how they can use the Christian armor this week. They should write in their notebooks what they believe God wants them to do.)

www.ingramcontent.com/pod-product-compliance
Lightning Source LLC
Chambersburg PA
CBHW060803090426
42736CB00002B/133